ADDRESS BOOK & TRACKER

_____

NAME

DATES: _____   _____
FROM   TO

This Christmas Card Tracker helps you stay organized and keeps track of all your Christmas card addresses in one place. You will be able to track your sent and received cards for up to six years.

This book has six pages per letter. Each letter is printed in the upper corner of each page allowing you to quickly flip through to find the contact you want. Each contact has a space for name, address, email, notes, and a space for sent/received tracking.

How To Use:

- For each contact, fill in the "20__" box with the current year.

- Tick or enter the date you sent the contact's card in the "Sent" box.

- Tick or enter the date you received the contact's card in the "Received" box.

A

Name		20____	20____	20____
Address	Sent?			
	Received?			

Email		20____	20____	20____
Notes	Sent?			
	Received?			

Name		20____	20____	20____
Address	Sent?			
	Received?			

Email		20____	20____	20____
Notes	Sent?			
	Received?			

Name		20____	20____	20____
Address	Sent?			
	Received?			

Email		20____	20____	20____
Notes	Sent?			
	Received?			

Name		20____	20____	20____
Address	Sent?			
	Received?			

Email		20____	20____	20____
Notes	Sent?			
	Received?			

Name		20___	20___	20___
Address	Sent?			
	Received?			
Email		20___	20___	20___
Notes	Sent?			
	Received?			

Name		20___	20___	20___
Address	Sent?			
	Received?			
Email		20___	20___	20___
Notes	Sent?			
	Received?			

Name		20___	20___	20___
Address	Sent?			
	Received?			
Email		20___	20___	20___
Notes	Sent?			
	Received?			

Name		20___	20___	20___
Address	Sent?			
	Received?			
Email		20___	20___	20___
Notes	Sent?			
	Received?			

A

Name		20____	20____	20____
Address	Sent?			
	Received?			
Email		20____	20____	20____
Notes	Sent?			
	Received?			

Name		20____	20____	20____
Address	Sent?			
	Received?			
Email		20____	20____	20____
Notes	Sent?			
	Received?			

Name		20____	20____	20____
Address	Sent?			
	Received?			
Email		20____	20____	20____
Notes	Sent?			
	Received?			

Name		20____	20____	20____
Address	Sent?			
	Received?			
Email		20____	20____	20____
Notes	Sent?			
	Received?			

Name		20____	20____	20____
Address	Sent?			
	Received?			
Email		20____	20____	20____
Notes	Sent?			
	Received?			

Name		20____	20____	20____
Address	Sent?			
	Received?			
Email		20____	20____	20____
Notes	Sent?			
	Received?			

Name		20____	20____	20____
Address	Sent?			
	Received?			
Email		20____	20____	20____
Notes	Sent?			
	Received?			

Name		20____	20____	20____
Address	Sent?			
	Received?			
Email		20____	20____	20____
Notes	Sent?			
	Received?			

A

Name			20____	20____	20____
Address		Sent?			
		Received?			

Email			20____	20____	20____
Notes		Sent?			
		Received?			

Name			20____	20____	20____
Address		Sent?			
		Received?			

Email			20____	20____	20____
Notes		Sent?			
		Received?			

Name			20____	20____	20____
Address		Sent?			
		Received?			

Email			20____	20____	20____
Notes		Sent?			
		Received?			

Name			20____	20____	20____
Address		Sent?			
		Received?			

Email			20____	20____	20____
Notes		Sent?			
		Received?			

Name		20_____	20_____	20_____
Address	Sent?			
	Received?			
Email		20_____	20_____	20_____
Notes	Sent?			
	Received?			

Name		20_____	20_____	20_____
Address	Sent?			
	Received?			
Email		20_____	20_____	20_____
Notes	Sent?			
	Received?			

Name		20_____	20_____	20_____
Address	Sent?			
	Received?			
Email		20_____	20_____	20_____
Notes	Sent?			
	Received?			

Name		20_____	20_____	20_____
Address	Sent?			
	Received?			
Email		20_____	20_____	20_____
Notes	Sent?			
	Received?			

B

Name		20____	20____	20____
Address	Sent?			
	Received?			
Email		20____	20____	20____
Notes	Sent?			
	Received?			

Name		20____	20____	20____
Address	Sent?			
	Received?			
Email		20____	20____	20____
Notes	Sent?			
	Received?			

Name		20____	20____	20____
Address	Sent?			
	Received?			
Email		20____	20____	20____
Notes	Sent?			
	Received?			

Name		20____	20____	20____
Address	Sent?			
	Received?			
Email		20____	20____	20____
Notes	Sent?			
	Received?			

Name		20____	20____	20____
Address	Sent?			
	Received?			
Email		20____	20____	20____
Notes	Sent?			
	Received?			

Name		20____	20____	20____
Address	Sent?			
	Received?			
Email		20____	20____	20____
Notes	Sent?			
	Received?			

Name		20____	20____	20____
Address	Sent?			
	Received?			
Email		20____	20____	20____
Notes	Sent?			
	Received?			

Name		20____	20____	20____
Address	Sent?			
	Received?			
Email		20____	20____	20____
Notes	Sent?			
	Received?			

B

Name		20____	20____	20____
Address	Sent?			
	Received?			
Email		20____	20____	20____
Notes	Sent?			
	Received?			

Name		20____	20____	20____
Address	Sent?			
	Received?			
Email		20____	20____	20____
Notes	Sent?			
	Received?			

Name		20____	20____	20____
Address	Sent?			
	Received?			
Email		20____	20____	20____
Notes	Sent?			
	Received?			

Name		20____	20____	20____
Address	Sent?			
	Received?			
Email		20____	20____	20____
Notes	Sent?			
	Received?			

Name		20____	20____	20____
Address	Sent?			
	Received?			
Email		20____	20____	20____
Notes	Sent?			
	Received?			

Name		20____	20____	20____
Address	Sent?			
	Received?			
Email		20____	20____	20____
Notes	Sent?			
	Received?			

Name		20____	20____	20____
Address	Sent?			
	Received?			
Email		20____	20____	20____
Notes	Sent?			
	Received?			

Name		20____	20____	20____
Address	Sent?			
	Received?			
Email		20____	20____	20____
Notes	Sent?			
	Received?			

B

Name		20____	20____	20____
Address	Sent?			
	Received?			
Email		20____	20____	20____
Notes	Sent?			
	Received?			

Name		20____	20____	20____
Address	Sent?			
	Received?			
Email		20____	20____	20____
Notes	Sent?			
	Received?			

Name		20____	20____	20____
Address	Sent?			
	Received?			
Email		20____	20____	20____
Notes	Sent?			
	Received?			

Name		20____	20____	20____
Address	Sent?			
	Received?			
Email		20____	20____	20____
Notes	Sent?			
	Received?			

Name		20____	20____	20____
Address	Sent?			
	Received?			
Email		20____	20____	20____
Notes	Sent?			
	Received?			

Name		20____	20____	20____
Address	Sent?			
	Received?			
Email		20____	20____	20____
Notes	Sent?			
	Received?			

Name		20____	20____	20____
Address	Sent?			
	Received?			
Email		20____	20____	20____
Notes	Sent?			
	Received?			

Name		20____	20____	20____
Address	Sent?			
	Received?			
Email		20____	20____	20____
Notes	Sent?			
	Received?			

C

Name		20____	20____	20____
Address	Sent?			
	Received?			
Email		20____	20____	20____
Notes	Sent?			
	Received?			

Name		20____	20____	20____
Address	Sent?			
	Received?			
Email		20____	20____	20____
Notes	Sent?			
	Received?			

Name		20____	20____	20____
Address	Sent?			
	Received?			
Email		20____	20____	20____
Notes	Sent?			
	Received?			

Name		20____	20____	20____
Address	Sent?			
	Received?			
Email		20____	20____	20____
Notes	Sent?			
	Received?			

Name		20____	20____	20____
Address	Sent?			
	Received?			
Email		20____	20____	20____
Notes	Sent?			
	Received?			

Name		20____	20____	20____
Address	Sent?			
	Received?			
Email		20____	20____	20____
Notes	Sent?			
	Received?			

Name		20____	20____	20____
Address	Sent?			
	Received?			
Email		20____	20____	20____
Notes	Sent?			
	Received?			

Name		20____	20____	20____
Address	Sent?			
	Received?			
Email		20____	20____	20____
Notes	Sent?			
	Received?			

C

Name		20____	20____	20____
Address	Sent?			
	Received?			
Email		20____	20____	20____
Notes	Sent?			
	Received?			

Name		20____	20____	20____
Address	Sent?			
	Received?			
Email		20____	20____	20____
Notes	Sent?			
	Received?			

Name		20____	20____	20____
Address	Sent?			
	Received?			
Email		20____	20____	20____
Notes	Sent?			
	Received?			

Name		20____	20____	20____
Address	Sent?			
	Received?			
Email		20____	20____	20____
Notes	Sent?			
	Received?			

Name		20____	20____	20____
Address	Sent?			
	Received?			
Email		20____	20____	20____
Notes	Sent?			
	Received?			

Name		20____	20____	20____
Address	Sent?			
	Received?			
Email		20____	20____	20____
Notes	Sent?			
	Received?			

Name		20____	20____	20____
Address	Sent?			
	Received?			
Email		20____	20____	20____
Notes	Sent?			
	Received?			

Name		20____	20____	20____
Address	Sent?			
	Received?			
Email		20____	20____	20____
Notes	Sent?			
	Received?			

C

Name		20____	20____	20____
Address	Sent?			
	Received?			
Email		20____	20____	20____
Notes	Sent?			
	Received?			

Name		20____	20____	20____
Address	Sent?			
	Received?			
Email		20____	20____	20____
Notes	Sent?			
	Received?			

Name		20____	20____	20____
Address	Sent?			
	Received?			
Email		20____	20____	20____
Notes	Sent?			
	Received?			

Name		20____	20____	20____
Address	Sent?			
	Received?			
Email		20____	20____	20____
Notes	Sent?			
	Received?			

Name		20____	20____	20____
Address	Sent?			
	Received?			
Email		20____	20____	20____
Notes	Sent?			
	Received?			

Name		20____	20____	20____
Address	Sent?			
	Received?			
Email		20____	20____	20____
Notes	Sent?			
	Received?			

Name		20____	20____	20____
Address	Sent?			
	Received?			
Email		20____	20____	20____
Notes	Sent?			
	Received?			

Name		20____	20____	20____
Address	Sent?			
	Received?			
Email		20____	20____	20____
Notes	Sent?			
	Received?			

D

Name		20___	20___	20___
Address	Sent?			
	Received?			
Email		20___	20___	20___
Notes	Sent?			
	Received?			

Name		20___	20___	20___
Address	Sent?			
	Received?			
Email		20___	20___	20___
Notes	Sent?			
	Received?			

Name		20___	20___	20___
Address	Sent?			
	Received?			
Email		20___	20___	20___
Notes	Sent?			
	Received?			

Name		20___	20___	20___
Address	Sent?			
	Received?			
Email		20___	20___	20___
Notes	Sent?			
	Received?			

Name		20____	20____	20____
Address	Sent?			
	Received?			
Email		20____	20____	20____
Notes	Sent?			
	Received?			

Name		20____	20____	20____
Address	Sent?			
	Received?			
Email		20____	20____	20____
Notes	Sent?			
	Received?			

Name		20____	20____	20____
Address	Sent?			
	Received?			
Email		20____	20____	20____
Notes	Sent?			
	Received?			

Name		20____	20____	20____
Address	Sent?			
	Received?			
Email		20____	20____	20____
Notes	Sent?			
	Received?			

D

Name		20____	20____	20____
Address	Sent?			
	Received?			
Email		20____	20____	20____
Notes	Sent?			
	Received?			

Name		20____	20____	20____
Address	Sent?			
	Received?			
Email		20____	20____	20____
Notes	Sent?			
	Received?			

Name		20____	20____	20____
Address	Sent?			
	Received?			
Email		20____	20____	20____
Notes	Sent?			
	Received?			

Name		20____	20____	20____
Address	Sent?			
	Received?			
Email		20____	20____	20____
Notes	Sent?			
	Received?			

Name		20____	20____	20____
Address	Sent?			
	Received?			
Email		20____	20____	20____
Notes	Sent?			
	Received?			

Name		20____	20____	20____
Address	Sent?			
	Received?			
Email		20____	20____	20____
Notes	Sent?			
	Received?			

Name		20____	20____	20____
Address	Sent?			
	Received?			
Email		20____	20____	20____
Notes	Sent?			
	Received?			

Name		20____	20____	20____
Address	Sent?			
	Received?			
Email		20____	20____	20____
Notes	Sent?			
	Received?			

D

Name		20____	20____	20____
Address	Sent?			
	Received?			
Email		20____	20____	20____
Notes	Sent?			
	Received?			

Name		20____	20____	20____
Address	Sent?			
	Received?			
Email		20____	20____	20____
Notes	Sent?			
	Received?			

Name		20____	20____	20____
Address	Sent?			
	Received?			
Email		20____	20____	20____
Notes	Sent?			
	Received?			

Name		20____	20____	20____
Address	Sent?			
	Received?			
Email		20____	20____	20____
Notes	Sent?			
	Received?			

D

Name		20____	20____	20____
Address	Sent?			
	Received?			
Email		20____	20____	20____
Notes	Sent?			
	Received?			

Name		20____	20____	20____
Address	Sent?			
	Received?			
Email		20____	20____	20____
Notes	Sent?			
	Received?			

Name		20____	20____	20____
Address	Sent?			
	Received?			
Email		20____	20____	20____
Notes	Sent?			
	Received?			

Name		20____	20____	20____
Address	Sent?			
	Received?			
Email		20____	20____	20____
Notes	Sent?			
	Received?			

E

Name		20___	20___	20___
Address	Sent?			
	Received?			

Email		20___	20___	20___
Notes	Sent?			
	Received?			

Name		20___	20___	20___
Address	Sent?			
	Received?			

Email		20___	20___	20___
Notes	Sent?			
	Received?			

Name		20___	20___	20___
Address	Sent?			
	Received?			

Email		20___	20___	20___
Notes	Sent?			
	Received?			

Name		20___	20___	20___
Address	Sent?			
	Received?			

Email		20___	20___	20___
Notes	Sent?			
	Received?			

E

Name		20____	20____	20____
Address	Sent?			
	Received?			
Email		20____	20____	20____
Notes	Sent?			
	Received?			

Name		20____	20____	20____
Address	Sent?			
	Received?			
Email		20____	20____	20____
Notes	Sent?			
	Received?			

Name		20____	20____	20____
Address	Sent?			
	Received?			
Email		20____	20____	20____
Notes	Sent?			
	Received?			

Name		20____	20____	20____
Address	Sent?			
	Received?			
Email		20____	20____	20____
Notes	Sent?			
	Received?			

E

Name		20____	20____	20____
Address	Sent?			
	Received?			
Email		20____	20____	20____
Notes	Sent?			
	Received?			

Name		20____	20____	20____
Address	Sent?			
	Received?			
Email		20____	20____	20____
Notes	Sent?			
	Received?			

Name		20____	20____	20____
Address	Sent?			
	Received?			
Email		20____	20____	20____
Notes	Sent?			
	Received?			

Name		20____	20____	20____
Address	Sent?			
	Received?			
Email		20____	20____	20____
Notes	Sent?			
	Received?			

Name		20___	20___	20___
Address	Sent?			
	Received?			
Email		20___	20___	20___
Notes	Sent?			
	Received?			

Name		20___	20___	20___
Address	Sent?			
	Received?			
Email		20___	20___	20___
Notes	Sent?			
	Received?			

Name		20___	20___	20___
Address	Sent?			
	Received?			
Email		20___	20___	20___
Notes	Sent?			
	Received?			

Name		20___	20___	20___
Address	Sent?			
	Received?			
Email		20___	20___	20___
Notes	Sent?			
	Received?			

E

Name		20___	20___	20___
Address	Sent?			
	Received?			
Email		20___	20___	20___
Notes	Sent?			
	Received?			

Name		20___	20___	20___
Address	Sent?			
	Received?			
Email		20___	20___	20___
Notes	Sent?			
	Received?			

Name		20___	20___	20___
Address	Sent?			
	Received?			
Email		20___	20___	20___
Notes	Sent?			
	Received?			

Name		20___	20___	20___
Address	Sent?			
	Received?			
Email		20___	20___	20___
Notes	Sent?			
	Received?			

E

Name		20___	20___	20___
Address	Sent?			
	Received?			
Email		20___	20___	20___
Notes	Sent?			
	Received?			

Name		20___	20___	20___
Address	Sent?			
	Received?			
Email		20___	20___	20___
Notes	Sent?			
	Received?			

Name		20___	20___	20___
Address	Sent?			
	Received?			
Email		20___	20___	20___
Notes	Sent?			
	Received?			

Name		20___	20___	20___
Address	Sent?			
	Received?			
Email		20___	20___	20___
Notes	Sent?			
	Received?			

F

Name		20____	20____	20____
Address	Sent?			
	Received?			
Email		20____	20____	20____
Notes	Sent?			
	Received?			

Name		20____	20____	20____
Address	Sent?			
	Received?			
Email		20____	20____	20____
Notes	Sent?			
	Received?			

Name		20____	20____	20____
Address	Sent?			
	Received?			
Email		20____	20____	20____
Notes	Sent?			
	Received?			

Name		20____	20____	20____
Address	Sent?			
	Received?			
Email		20____	20____	20____
Notes	Sent?			
	Received?			

F

Name			20____	20____	20____
Address		Sent?			
		Received?			
Email			20____	20____	20____
Notes		Sent?			
		Received?			

Name			20____	20____	20____
Address		Sent?			
		Received?			
Email			20____	20____	20____
Notes		Sent?			
		Received?			

Name			20____	20____	20____
Address		Sent?			
		Received?			
Email			20____	20____	20____
Notes		Sent?			
		Received?			

Name			20____	20____	20____
Address		Sent?			
		Received?			
Email			20____	20____	20____
Notes		Sent?			
		Received?			

F

Name		20____	20____	20____
Address	Sent?			
	Received?			
Email		20____	20____	20____
Notes	Sent?			
	Received?			

Name		20____	20____	20____
Address	Sent?			
	Received?			
Email		20____	20____	20____
Notes	Sent?			
	Received?			

Name		20____	20____	20____
Address	Sent?			
	Received?			
Email		20____	20____	20____
Notes	Sent?			
	Received?			

Name		20____	20____	20____
Address	Sent?			
	Received?			
Email		20____	20____	20____
Notes	Sent?			
	Received?			

Name		20___	20___	20___
Address	Sent?			
	Received?			
Email		20___	20___	20___
Notes	Sent?			
	Received?			

Name		20___	20___	20___
Address	Sent?			
	Received?			
Email		20___	20___	20___
Notes	Sent?			
	Received?			

Name		20___	20___	20___
Address	Sent?			
	Received?			
Email		20___	20___	20___
Notes	Sent?			
	Received?			

Name		20___	20___	20___
Address	Sent?			
	Received?			
Email		20___	20___	20___
Notes	Sent?			
	Received?			

F

Name		20_____	20_____	20_____
Address	Sent?			
	Received?			
Email		20_____	20_____	20_____
Notes	Sent?			
	Received?			

Name		20_____	20_____	20_____
Address	Sent?			
	Received?			
Email		20_____	20_____	20_____
Notes	Sent?			
	Received?			

Name		20_____	20_____	20_____
Address	Sent?			
	Received?			
Email		20_____	20_____	20_____
Notes	Sent?			
	Received?			

Name		20_____	20_____	20_____
Address	Sent?			
	Received?			
Email		20_____	20_____	20_____
Notes	Sent?			
	Received?			

Name		20____	20____	20____
Address	Sent?			
	Received?			
Email		20____	20____	20____
Notes	Sent?			
	Received?			

Name		20____	20____	20____
Address	Sent?			
	Received?			
Email		20____	20____	20____
Notes	Sent?			
	Received?			

Name		20____	20____	20____
Address	Sent?			
	Received?			
Email		20____	20____	20____
Notes	Sent?			
	Received?			

Name		20____	20____	20____
Address	Sent?			
	Received?			
Email		20____	20____	20____
Notes	Sent?			
	Received?			

G

Name		20____	20____	20____
Address	Sent?			
	Received?			
Email		20____	20____	20____
Notes	Sent?			
	Received?			

Name		20____	20____	20____
Address	Sent?			
	Received?			
Email		20____	20____	20____
Notes	Sent?			
	Received?			

Name		20____	20____	20____
Address	Sent?			
	Received?			
Email		20____	20____	20____
Notes	Sent?			
	Received?			

Name		20____	20____	20____
Address	Sent?			
	Received?			
Email		20____	20____	20____
Notes	Sent?			
	Received?			

Name	20____	20____	20____
Address	Sent?			
	Received?			
Email	20____	20____	20____
Notes	Sent?			
	Received?			

Name	20____	20____	20____
Address	Sent?			
	Received?			
Email	20____	20____	20____
Notes	Sent?			
	Received?			

Name	20____	20____	20____
Address	Sent?			
	Received?			
Email	20____	20____	20____
Notes	Sent?			
	Received?			

Name	20____	20____	20____
Address	Sent?			
	Received?			
Email	20____	20____	20____
Notes	Sent?			
	Received?			

G

Name		20____	20____	20____
Address	Sent?			
	Received?			
Email		20____	20____	20____
Notes	Sent?			
	Received?			

Name		20____	20____	20____
Address	Sent?			
	Received?			
Email		20____	20____	20____
Notes	Sent?			
	Received?			

Name		20____	20____	20____
Address	Sent?			
	Received?			
Email		20____	20____	20____
Notes	Sent?			
	Received?			

Name		20____	20____	20____
Address	Sent?			
	Received?			
Email		20____	20____	20____
Notes	Sent?			
	Received?			

Name			20____	20____	20____
Address		Sent?			
		Received?			
Email			20____	20____	20____
Notes		Sent?			
		Received?			

Name			20____	20____	20____
Address		Sent?			
		Received?			
Email			20____	20____	20____
Notes		Sent?			
		Received?			

Name			20____	20____	20____
Address		Sent?			
		Received?			
Email			20____	20____	20____
Notes		Sent?			
		Received?			

Name			20____	20____	20____
Address		Sent?			
		Received?			
Email			20____	20____	20____
Notes		Sent?			
		Received?			

G

Name		20____	20____	20____
Address	Sent?			
	Received?			

Email		20____	20____	20____
Notes	Sent?			
	Received?			

Name		20____	20____	20____
Address	Sent?			
	Received?			

Email		20____	20____	20____
Notes	Sent?			
	Received?			

Name		20____	20____	20____
Address	Sent?			
	Received?			

Email		20____	20____	20____
Notes	Sent?			
	Received?			

Name		20____	20____	20____
Address	Sent?			
	Received?			

Email		20____	20____	20____
Notes	Sent?			
	Received?			

G

Name		20____	20____	20____
Address	Sent?			
	Received?			
Email		20____	20____	20____
Notes	Sent?			
	Received?			

Name		20____	20____	20____
Address	Sent?			
	Received?			
Email		20____	20____	20____
Notes	Sent?			
	Received?			

Name		20____	20____	20____
Address	Sent?			
	Received?			
Email		20____	20____	20____
Notes	Sent?			
	Received?			

Name		20____	20____	20____
Address	Sent?			
	Received?			
Email		20____	20____	20____
Notes	Sent?			
	Received?			

H

Name		20____	20____	20____
Address	Sent?			
	Received?			
Email		20____	20____	20____
Notes	Sent?			
	Received?			

Name		20____	20____	20____
Address	Sent?			
	Received?			
Email		20____	20____	20____
Notes	Sent?			
	Received?			

Name		20____	20____	20____
Address	Sent?			
	Received?			
Email		20____	20____	20____
Notes	Sent?			
	Received?			

Name		20____	20____	20____
Address	Sent?			
	Received?			
Email		20____	20____	20____
Notes	Sent?			
	Received?			

H

Name	20___	20___	20___
Address	Sent?			
	Received?			

Email	20___	20___	20___
Notes	Sent?			
	Received?			

Name	20___	20___	20___
Address	Sent?			
	Received?			

Email	20___	20___	20___
Notes	Sent?			
	Received?			

Name	20___	20___	20___
Address	Sent?			
	Received?			

Email	20___	20___	20___
Notes	Sent?			
	Received?			

Name	20___	20___	20___
Address	Sent?			
	Received?			

Email	20___	20___	20___
Notes	Sent?			
	Received?			

H

Name		20____	20____	20____
Address	Sent?			
	Received?			
Email		20____	20____	20____
Notes	Sent?			
	Received?			

Name		20____	20____	20____
Address	Sent?			
	Received?			
Email		20____	20____	20____
Notes	Sent?			
	Received?			

Name		20____	20____	20____
Address	Sent?			
	Received?			
Email		20____	20____	20____
Notes	Sent?			
	Received?			

Name		20____	20____	20____
Address	Sent?			
	Received?			
Email		20____	20____	20____
Notes	Sent?			
	Received?			

Name		20____	20____	20____
Address	Sent?			
	Received?			
Email		20____	20____	20____
Notes	Sent?			
	Received?			

Name		20____	20____	20____
Address	Sent?			
	Received?			
Email		20____	20____	20____
Notes	Sent?			
	Received?			

Name		20____	20____	20____
Address	Sent?			
	Received?			
Email		20____	20____	20____
Notes	Sent?			
	Received?			

Name		20____	20____	20____
Address	Sent?			
	Received?			
Email		20____	20____	20____
Notes	Sent?			
	Received?			

H

Name		20____	20____	20____
Address	Sent?			
	Received?			
Email		20____	20____	20____
Notes	Sent?			
	Received?			

Name		20____	20____	20____
Address	Sent?			
	Received?			
Email		20____	20____	20____
Notes	Sent?			
	Received?			

Name		20____	20____	20____
Address	Sent?			
	Received?			
Email		20____	20____	20____
Notes	Sent?			
	Received?			

Name		20____	20____	20____
Address	Sent?			
	Received?			
Email		20____	20____	20____
Notes	Sent?			
	Received?			

H

Name		20___	20___	20___
Address	Sent?			
	Received?			
Email		20___	20___	20___
Notes	Sent?			
	Received?			

Name		20___	20___	20___
Address	Sent?			
	Received?			
Email		20___	20___	20___
Notes	Sent?			
	Received?			

Name		20___	20___	20___
Address	Sent?			
	Received?			
Email		20___	20___	20___
Notes	Sent?			
	Received?			

Name		20___	20___	20___
Address	Sent?			
	Received?			
Email		20___	20___	20___
Notes	Sent?			
	Received?			

I

Name		20____	20____	20____
Address	Sent?			
	Received?			
Email		20____	20____	20____
Notes	Sent?			
	Received?			

Name		20____	20____	20____
Address	Sent?			
	Received?			
Email		20____	20____	20____
Notes	Sent?			
	Received?			

Name		20____	20____	20____
Address	Sent?			
	Received?			
Email		20____	20____	20____
Notes	Sent?			
	Received?			

Name		20____	20____	20____
Address	Sent?			
	Received?			
Email		20____	20____	20____
Notes	Sent?			
	Received?			

Name		20___	20___	20___
Address	Sent?			
	Received?			
Email		20___	20___	20___
Notes	Sent?			
	Received?			

Name		20___	20___	20___
Address	Sent?			
	Received?			
Email		20___	20___	20___
Notes	Sent?			
	Received?			

Name		20___	20___	20___
Address	Sent?			
	Received?			
Email		20___	20___	20___
Notes	Sent?			
	Received?			

Name		20___	20___	20___
Address	Sent?			
	Received?			
Email		20___	20___	20___
Notes	Sent?			
	Received?			

I

Name		20____	20____	20____
Address	Sent?			
	Received?			
Email		20____	20____	20____
Notes	Sent?			
	Received?			

Name		20____	20____	20____
Address	Sent?			
	Received?			
Email		20____	20____	20____
Notes	Sent?			
	Received?			

Name		20____	20____	20____
Address	Sent?			
	Received?			
Email		20____	20____	20____
Notes	Sent?			
	Received?			

Name		20____	20____	20____
Address	Sent?			
	Received?			
Email		20____	20____	20____
Notes	Sent?			
	Received?			

I

Name		20____	20____	20____
Address	Sent?			
	Received?			
Email		20____	20____	20____
Notes	Sent?			
	Received?			

Name		20____	20____	20____
Address	Sent?			
	Received?			
Email		20____	20____	20____
Notes	Sent?			
	Received?			

Name		20____	20____	20____
Address	Sent?			
	Received?			
Email		20____	20____	20____
Notes	Sent?			
	Received?			

Name		20____	20____	20____
Address	Sent?			
	Received?			
Email		20____	20____	20____
Notes	Sent?			
	Received?			

I

Name		20____	20____	20____
Address	Sent?			
	Received?			
Email		20____	20____	20____
Notes	Sent?			
	Received?			

Name		20____	20____	20____
Address	Sent?			
	Received?			
Email		20____	20____	20____
Notes	Sent?			
	Received?			

Name		20____	20____	20____
Address	Sent?			
	Received?			
Email		20____	20____	20____
Notes	Sent?			
	Received?			

Name		20____	20____	20____
Address	Sent?			
	Received?			
Email		20____	20____	20____
Notes	Sent?			
	Received?			

Name		20____	20____	20____
Address	Sent?			
	Received?			
Email		20____	20____	20____
Notes	Sent?			
	Received?			

Name		20____	20____	20____
Address	Sent?			
	Received?			
Email		20____	20____	20____
Notes	Sent?			
	Received?			

Name		20____	20____	20____
Address	Sent?			
	Received?			
Email		20____	20____	20____
Notes	Sent?			
	Received?			

Name		20____	20____	20____
Address	Sent?			
	Received?			
Email		20____	20____	20____
Notes	Sent?			
	Received?			

J

Name		20____	20____	20____
Address	Sent?			
	Received?			
Email		20____	20____	20____
Notes	Sent?			
	Received?			

Name		20____	20____	20____
Address	Sent?			
	Received?			
Email		20____	20____	20____
Notes	Sent?			
	Received?			

Name		20____	20____	20____
Address	Sent?			
	Received?			
Email		20____	20____	20____
Notes	Sent?			
	Received?			

Name		20____	20____	20____
Address	Sent?			
	Received?			
Email		20____	20____	20____
Notes	Sent?			
	Received?			

Name		20___	20___	20___
Address	Sent?			
	Received?			
Email		20___	20___	20___
Notes	Sent?			
	Received?			

Name		20___	20___	20___
Address	Sent?			
	Received?			
Email		20___	20___	20___
Notes	Sent?			
	Received?			

Name		20___	20___	20___
Address	Sent?			
	Received?			
Email		20___	20___	20___
Notes	Sent?			
	Received?			

Name		20___	20___	20___
Address	Sent?			
	Received?			
Email		20___	20___	20___
Notes	Sent?			
	Received?			

J

Name		20___	20___	20___
Address	Sent?			
	Received?			
Email		20___	20___	20___
Notes	Sent?			
	Received?			

Name		20___	20___	20___
Address	Sent?			
	Received?			
Email		20___	20___	20___
Notes	Sent?			
	Received?			

Name		20___	20___	20___
Address	Sent?			
	Received?			
Email		20___	20___	20___
Notes	Sent?			
	Received?			

Name		20___	20___	20___
Address	Sent?			
	Received?			
Email		20___	20___	20___
Notes	Sent?			
	Received?			

Name		20_____	20_____	20_____
Address	Sent?			
	Received?			
Email		20_____	20_____	20_____
Notes	Sent?			
	Received?			

Name		20_____	20_____	20_____
Address	Sent?			
	Received?			
Email		20_____	20_____	20_____
Notes	Sent?			
	Received?			

Name		20_____	20_____	20_____
Address	Sent?			
	Received?			
Email		20_____	20_____	20_____
Notes	Sent?			
	Received?			

Name		20_____	20_____	20_____
Address	Sent?			
	Received?			
Email		20_____	20_____	20_____
Notes	Sent?			
	Received?			

J

Name	20____	20____	20____
Address	Sent?			
	Received?			

Email	20____	20____	20____
Notes	Sent?			
	Received?			

Name	20____	20____	20____
Address	Sent?			
	Received?			

Email	20____	20____	20____
Notes	Sent?			
	Received?			

Name	20____	20____	20____
Address	Sent?			
	Received?			

Email	20____	20____	20____
Notes	Sent?			
	Received?			

Name	20____	20____	20____
Address	Sent?			
	Received?			

Email	20____	20____	20____
Notes	Sent?			
	Received?			

J

Name		20___	20___	20___
Address	Sent?			
	Received?			
Email		20___	20___	20___
Notes	Sent?			
	Received?			

Name		20___	20___	20___
Address	Sent?			
	Received?			
Email		20___	20___	20___
Notes	Sent?			
	Received?			

Name		20___	20___	20___
Address	Sent?			
	Received?			
Email		20___	20___	20___
Notes	Sent?			
	Received?			

Name		20___	20___	20___
Address	Sent?			
	Received?			
Email		20___	20___	20___
Notes	Sent?			
	Received?			

K

Name		20____	20____	20____
Address	Sent?			
	Received?			
Email		20____	20____	20____
Notes	Sent?			
	Received?			

Name		20____	20____	20____
Address	Sent?			
	Received?			
Email		20____	20____	20____
Notes	Sent?			
	Received?			

Name		20____	20____	20____
Address	Sent?			
	Received?			
Email		20____	20____	20____
Notes	Sent?			
	Received?			

Name		20____	20____	20____
Address	Sent?			
	Received?			
Email		20____	20____	20____
Notes	Sent?			
	Received?			

Name		20___	20___	20___
Address	Sent?			
	Received?			
Email		20___	20___	20___
Notes	Sent?			
	Received?			

Name		20___	20___	20___
Address	Sent?			
	Received?			
Email		20___	20___	20___
Notes	Sent?			
	Received?			

Name		20___	20___	20___
Address	Sent?			
	Received?			
Email		20___	20___	20___
Notes	Sent?			
	Received?			

Name		20___	20___	20___
Address	Sent?			
	Received?			
Email		20___	20___	20___
Notes	Sent?			
	Received?			

K

Name		20____	20____	20____
Address	Sent?			
	Received?			
Email		20____	20____	20____
Notes	Sent?			
	Received?			

Name		20____	20____	20____
Address	Sent?			
	Received?			
Email		20____	20____	20____
Notes	Sent?			
	Received?			

Name		20____	20____	20____
Address	Sent?			
	Received?			
Email		20____	20____	20____
Notes	Sent?			
	Received?			

Name		20____	20____	20____
Address	Sent?			
	Received?			
Email		20____	20____	20____
Notes	Sent?			
	Received?			

Name		20____	20____	20____
Address	Sent?			
	Received?			
Email		20____	20____	20____
Notes	Sent?			
	Received?			

Name		20____	20____	20____
Address	Sent?			
	Received?			
Email		20____	20____	20____
Notes	Sent?			
	Received?			

Name		20____	20____	20____
Address	Sent?			
	Received?			
Email		20____	20____	20____
Notes	Sent?			
	Received?			

Name		20____	20____	20____
Address	Sent?			
	Received?			
Email		20____	20____	20____
Notes	Sent?			
	Received?			

K

Name		20____	20____	20____
Address	Sent?			
	Received?			
Email		20____	20____	20____
Notes	Sent?			
	Received?			

Name		20____	20____	20____
Address	Sent?			
	Received?			
Email		20____	20____	20____
Notes	Sent?			
	Received?			

Name		20____	20____	20____
Address	Sent?			
	Received?			
Email		20____	20____	20____
Notes	Sent?			
	Received?			

Name		20____	20____	20____
Address	Sent?			
	Received?			
Email		20____	20____	20____
Notes	Sent?			
	Received?			

Name		20_____	20_____	20_____
Address	Sent?			
	Received?			
Email		20_____	20_____	20_____
Notes	Sent?			
	Received?			

Name		20_____	20_____	20_____
Address	Sent?			
	Received?			
Email		20_____	20_____	20_____
Notes	Sent?			
	Received?			

Name		20_____	20_____	20_____
Address	Sent?			
	Received?			
Email		20_____	20_____	20_____
Notes	Sent?			
	Received?			

Name		20_____	20_____	20_____
Address	Sent?			
	Received?			
Email		20_____	20_____	20_____
Notes	Sent?			
	Received?			

L

Name		20____	20____	20____
Address	Sent?			
	Received?			
Email		20____	20____	20____
Notes	Sent?			
	Received?			

Name		20____	20____	20____
Address	Sent?			
	Received?			
Email		20____	20____	20____
Notes	Sent?			
	Received?			

Name		20____	20____	20____
Address	Sent?			
	Received?			
Email		20____	20____	20____
Notes	Sent?			
	Received?			

Name		20____	20____	20____
Address	Sent?			
	Received?			
Email		20____	20____	20____
Notes	Sent?			
	Received?			

Name		20____	20____	20____
Address	Sent?			
	Received?			
Email		20____	20____	20____
Notes	Sent?			
	Received?			

Name		20____	20____	20____
Address	Sent?			
	Received?			
Email		20____	20____	20____
Notes	Sent?			
	Received?			

Name		20____	20____	20____
Address	Sent?			
	Received?			
Email		20____	20____	20____
Notes	Sent?			
	Received?			

Name		20____	20____	20____
Address	Sent?			
	Received?			
Email		20____	20____	20____
Notes	Sent?			
	Received?			

L

Name		20____	20____	20____
Address	Sent?			
	Received?			
Email		20____	20____	20____
Notes	Sent?			
	Received?			

Name		20____	20____	20____
Address	Sent?			
	Received?			
Email		20____	20____	20____
Notes	Sent?			
	Received?			

Name		20____	20____	20____
Address	Sent?			
	Received?			
Email		20____	20____	20____
Notes	Sent?			
	Received?			

Name		20____	20____	20____
Address	Sent?			
	Received?			
Email		20____	20____	20____
Notes	Sent?			
	Received?			

Name		20____	20____	20____
Address	Sent?			
	Received?			
Email		20____	20____	20____
Notes	Sent?			
	Received?			

Name		20____	20____	20____
Address	Sent?			
	Received?			
Email		20____	20____	20____
Notes	Sent?			
	Received?			

Name		20____	20____	20____
Address	Sent?			
	Received?			
Email		20____	20____	20____
Notes	Sent?			
	Received?			

Name		20____	20____	20____
Address	Sent?			
	Received?			
Email		20____	20____	20____
Notes	Sent?			
	Received?			

L

Name		20___	20___	20___
Address	Sent?			
	Received?			
Email		20___	20___	20___
Notes	Sent?			
	Received?			

Name		20___	20___	20___
Address	Sent?			
	Received?			
Email		20___	20___	20___
Notes	Sent?			
	Received?			

Name		20___	20___	20___
Address	Sent?			
	Received?			
Email		20___	20___	20___
Notes	Sent?			
	Received?			

Name		20___	20___	20___
Address	Sent?			
	Received?			
Email		20___	20___	20___
Notes	Sent?			
	Received?			

Name		20____	20____	20____
Address	Sent?			
	Received?			
Email		20____	20____	20____
Notes	Sent?			
	Received?			

Name		20____	20____	20____
Address	Sent?			
	Received?			
Email		20____	20____	20____
Notes	Sent?			
	Received?			

Name		20____	20____	20____
Address	Sent?			
	Received?			
Email		20____	20____	20____
Notes	Sent?			
	Received?			

Name		20____	20____	20____
Address	Sent?			
	Received?			
Email		20____	20____	20____
Notes	Sent?			
	Received?			

M

Name		20____	20____	20____
Address	Sent?			
	Received?			
Email		20____	20____	20____
Notes	Sent?			
	Received?			

Name		20____	20____	20____
Address	Sent?			
	Received?			
Email		20____	20____	20____
Notes	Sent?			
	Received?			

Name		20____	20____	20____
Address	Sent?			
	Received?			
Email		20____	20____	20____
Notes	Sent?			
	Received?			

Name		20____	20____	20____
Address	Sent?			
	Received?			
Email		20____	20____	20____
Notes	Sent?			
	Received?			

M

Name		20____	20____	20____
Address	Sent?			
	Received?			
Email		20____	20____	20____
Notes	Sent?			
	Received?			

Name		20____	20____	20____
Address	Sent?			
	Received?			
Email		20____	20____	20____
Notes	Sent?			
	Received?			

Name		20____	20____	20____
Address	Sent?			
	Received?			
Email		20____	20____	20____
Notes	Sent?			
	Received?			

Name		20____	20____	20____
Address	Sent?			
	Received?			
Email		20____	20____	20____
Notes	Sent?			
	Received?			

M

Name		20___	20___	20___
Address	Sent?			
	Received?			
Email		20___	20___	20___
Notes	Sent?			
	Received?			

Name		20___	20___	20___
Address	Sent?			
	Received?			
Email		20___	20___	20___
Notes	Sent?			
	Received?			

Name		20___	20___	20___
Address	Sent?			
	Received?			
Email		20___	20___	20___
Notes	Sent?			
	Received?			

Name		20___	20___	20___
Address	Sent?			
	Received?			
Email		20___	20___	20___
Notes	Sent?			
	Received?			

M

Name		20___	20___	20___
Address	Sent?			
	Received?			
Email		20___	20___	20___
Notes	Sent?			
	Received?			

Name		20___	20___	20___
Address	Sent?			
	Received?			
Email		20___	20___	20___
Notes	Sent?			
	Received?			

Name		20___	20___	20___
Address	Sent?			
	Received?			
Email		20___	20___	20___
Notes	Sent?			
	Received?			

Name		20___	20___	20___
Address	Sent?			
	Received?			
Email		20___	20___	20___
Notes	Sent?			
	Received?			

M

Name		20____	20____	20____
Address	Sent?			
	Received?			
Email		20____	20____	20____
Notes	Sent?			
	Received?			

Name		20____	20____	20____
Address	Sent?			
	Received?			
Email		20____	20____	20____
Notes	Sent?			
	Received?			

Name		20____	20____	20____
Address	Sent?			
	Received?			
Email		20____	20____	20____
Notes	Sent?			
	Received?			

Name		20____	20____	20____
Address	Sent?			
	Received?			
Email		20____	20____	20____
Notes	Sent?			
	Received?			

M

Name	20____	20____	20____
Address	Sent?			
	Received?			

Email	20____	20____	20____
Notes	Sent?			
	Received?			

Name	20____	20____	20____
Address	Sent?			
	Received?			

Email	20____	20____	20____
Notes	Sent?			
	Received?			

Name	20____	20____	20____
Address	Sent?			
	Received?			

Email	20____	20____	20____
Notes	Sent?			
	Received?			

Name	20____	20____	20____
Address	Sent?			
	Received?			

Email	20____	20____	20____
Notes	Sent?			
	Received?			

N

Name		20___	20___	20___
Address	Sent?			
	Received?			

Email		20___	20___	20___
Notes	Sent?			
	Received?			

Name		20___	20___	20___
Address	Sent?			
	Received?			

Email		20___	20___	20___
Notes	Sent?			
	Received?			

Name		20___	20___	20___
Address	Sent?			
	Received?			

Email		20___	20___	20___
Notes	Sent?			
	Received?			

Name		20___	20___	20___
Address	Sent?			
	Received?			

Email		20___	20___	20___
Notes	Sent?			
	Received?			

Name		20____	20____	20____
Address	Sent?			
	Received?			
Email		20____	20____	20____
Notes	Sent?			
	Received?			

Name		20____	20____	20____
Address	Sent?			
	Received?			
Email		20____	20____	20____
Notes	Sent?			
	Received?			

Name		20____	20____	20____
Address	Sent?			
	Received?			
Email		20____	20____	20____
Notes	Sent?			
	Received?			

Name		20____	20____	20____
Address	Sent?			
	Received?			
Email		20____	20____	20____
Notes	Sent?			
	Received?			

N

Name		20____	20____	20____
Address	Sent?			
	Received?			
Email		20____	20____	20____
Notes	Sent?			
	Received?			

Name		20____	20____	20____
Address	Sent?			
	Received?			
Email		20____	20____	20____
Notes	Sent?			
	Received?			

Name		20____	20____	20____
Address	Sent?			
	Received?			
Email		20____	20____	20____
Notes	Sent?			
	Received?			

Name		20____	20____	20____
Address	Sent?			
	Received?			
Email		20____	20____	20____
Notes	Sent?			
	Received?			

Name		20____	20____	20____
Address	Sent?			
	Received?			
Email		20____	20____	20____
Notes	Sent?			
	Received?			

Name		20____	20____	20____
Address	Sent?			
	Received?			
Email		20____	20____	20____
Notes	Sent?			
	Received?			

Name		20____	20____	20____
Address	Sent?			
	Received?			
Email		20____	20____	20____
Notes	Sent?			
	Received?			

Name		20____	20____	20____
Address	Sent?			
	Received?			
Email		20____	20____	20____
Notes	Sent?			
	Received?			

N

Name		20____	20____	20____
Address	Sent?			
	Received?			
Email		20____	20____	20____
Notes	Sent?			
	Received?			

Name		20____	20____	20____
Address	Sent?			
	Received?			
Email		20____	20____	20____
Notes	Sent?			
	Received?			

Name		20____	20____	20____
Address	Sent?			
	Received?			
Email		20____	20____	20____
Notes	Sent?			
	Received?			

Name		20____	20____	20____
Address	Sent?			
	Received?			
Email		20____	20____	20____
Notes	Sent?			
	Received?			

Name		20___	20___	20___
Address	Sent?			
	Received?			
Email		20___	20___	20___
Notes	Sent?			
	Received?			

Name		20___	20___	20___
Address	Sent?			
	Received?			
Email		20___	20___	20___
Notes	Sent?			
	Received?			

Name		20___	20___	20___
Address	Sent?			
	Received?			
Email		20___	20___	20___
Notes	Sent?			
	Received?			

Name		20___	20___	20___
Address	Sent?			
	Received?			
Email		20___	20___	20___
Notes	Sent?			
	Received?			

O

Name		20____	20____	20____
Address	Sent?			
	Received?			

Email		20____	20____	20____
Notes	Sent?			
	Received?			

Name		20____	20____	20____
Address	Sent?			
	Received?			

Email		20____	20____	20____
Notes	Sent?			
	Received?			

Name		20____	20____	20____
Address	Sent?			
	Received?			

Email		20____	20____	20____
Notes	Sent?			
	Received?			

Name		20____	20____	20____
Address	Sent?			
	Received?			

Email		20____	20____	20____
Notes	Sent?			
	Received?			

O

		20____	20____	20____
Name				
Address	Sent?			
	Received?			
		20____	20____	20____
Email				
Notes	Sent?			
	Received?			

		20____	20____	20____
Name				
Address	Sent?			
	Received?			
		20____	20____	20____
Email				
Notes	Sent?			
	Received?			

		20____	20____	20____
Name				
Address	Sent?			
	Received?			
		20____	20____	20____
Email				
Notes	Sent?			
	Received?			

		20____	20____	20____
Name				
Address	Sent?			
	Received?			
		20____	20____	20____
Email				
Notes	Sent?			
	Received?			

O

Name		20_____	20_____	20_____
Address	Sent?			
	Received?			
Email		20_____	20_____	20_____
Notes	Sent?			
	Received?			

Name		20_____	20_____	20_____
Address	Sent?			
	Received?			
Email		20_____	20_____	20_____
Notes	Sent?			
	Received?			

Name		20_____	20_____	20_____
Address	Sent?			
	Received?			
Email		20_____	20_____	20_____
Notes	Sent?			
	Received?			

Name		20_____	20_____	20_____
Address	Sent?			
	Received?			
Email		20_____	20_____	20_____
Notes	Sent?			
	Received?			

O

		20____	20____	20____
Name				
Address	Sent?			
	Received?			
Email		20____	20____	20____
Notes	Sent?			
	Received?			

		20____	20____	20____
Name				
Address	Sent?			
	Received?			
Email		20____	20____	20____
Notes	Sent?			
	Received?			

		20____	20____	20____
Name				
Address	Sent?			
	Received?			
Email		20____	20____	20____
Notes	Sent?			
	Received?			

		20____	20____	20____
Name				
Address	Sent?			
	Received?			
Email		20____	20____	20____
Notes	Sent?			
	Received?			

O

Name		20___	20___	20___
Address	Sent?			
	Received?			

Email		20___	20___	20___
Notes	Sent?			
	Received?			

Name		20___	20___	20___
Address	Sent?			
	Received?			

Email		20___	20___	20___
Notes	Sent?			
	Received?			

Name		20___	20___	20___
Address	Sent?			
	Received?			

Email		20___	20___	20___
Notes	Sent?			
	Received?			

Name		20___	20___	20___
Address	Sent?			
	Received?			

Email		20___	20___	20___
Notes	Sent?			
	Received?			

Name		20____	20____	20____
Address	Sent?			
	Received?			
Email		20____	20____	20____
Notes	Sent?			
	Received?			

Name		20____	20____	20____
Address	Sent?			
	Received?			
Email		20____	20____	20____
Notes	Sent?			
	Received?			

Name		20____	20____	20____
Address	Sent?			
	Received?			
Email		20____	20____	20____
Notes	Sent?			
	Received?			

Name		20____	20____	20____
Address	Sent?			
	Received?			
Email		20____	20____	20____
Notes	Sent?			
	Received?			

P

Name	20____	20____	20____
Address	Sent?			
	Received?			

Email	20____	20____	20____
Notes	Sent?			
	Received?			

Name	20____	20____	20____
Address	Sent?			
	Received?			

Email	20____	20____	20____
Notes	Sent?			
	Received?			

Name	20____	20____	20____
Address	Sent?			
	Received?			

Email	20____	20____	20____
Notes	Sent?			
	Received?			

Name	20____	20____	20____
Address	Sent?			
	Received?			

Email	20____	20____	20____
Notes	Sent?			
	Received?			

Name		20___	20___	20___
Address	Sent?			
	Received?			
Email		20___	20___	20___
Notes	Sent?			
	Received?			

Name		20___	20___	20___
Address	Sent?			
	Received?			
Email		20___	20___	20___
Notes	Sent?			
	Received?			

Name		20___	20___	20___
Address	Sent?			
	Received?			
Email		20___	20___	20___
Notes	Sent?			
	Received?			

Name		20___	20___	20___
Address	Sent?			
	Received?			
Email		20___	20___	20___
Notes	Sent?			
	Received?			

P

Name		20____	20____	20____
Address	Sent?			
	Received?			
Email		20____	20____	20____
Notes	Sent?			
	Received?			

Name		20____	20____	20____
Address	Sent?			
	Received?			
Email		20____	20____	20____
Notes	Sent?			
	Received?			

Name		20____	20____	20____
Address	Sent?			
	Received?			
Email		20____	20____	20____
Notes	Sent?			
	Received?			

Name		20____	20____	20____
Address	Sent?			
	Received?			
Email		20____	20____	20____
Notes	Sent?			
	Received?			

Name		20___	20___	20___
Address	Sent?			
	Received?			
Email		20___	20___	20___
Notes	Sent?			
	Received?			

Name		20___	20___	20___
Address	Sent?			
	Received?			
Email		20___	20___	20___
Notes	Sent?			
	Received?			

Name		20___	20___	20___
Address	Sent?			
	Received?			
Email		20___	20___	20___
Notes	Sent?			
	Received?			

Name		20___	20___	20___
Address	Sent?			
	Received?			
Email		20___	20___	20___
Notes	Sent?			
	Received?			

P

Name		20____	20____	20____
Address	Sent?			
	Received?			
Email		20____	20____	20____
Notes	Sent?			
	Received?			

Name		20____	20____	20____
Address	Sent?			
	Received?			
Email		20____	20____	20____
Notes	Sent?			
	Received?			

Name		20____	20____	20____
Address	Sent?			
	Received?			
Email		20____	20____	20____
Notes	Sent?			
	Received?			

Name		20____	20____	20____
Address	Sent?			
	Received?			
Email		20____	20____	20____
Notes	Sent?			
	Received?			

Name		20____	20____	20____
Address	Sent?			
	Received?			
Email		20____	20____	20____
Notes	Sent?			
	Received?			

Name		20____	20____	20____
Address	Sent?			
	Received?			
Email		20____	20____	20____
Notes	Sent?			
	Received?			

Name		20____	20____	20____
Address	Sent?			
	Received?			
Email		20____	20____	20____
Notes	Sent?			
	Received?			

Name		20____	20____	20____
Address	Sent?			
	Received?			
Email		20____	20____	20____
Notes	Sent?			
	Received?			

Q

Name		20____	20____	20____
Address	Sent?			
	Received?			

Email		20____	20____	20____
Notes	Sent?			
	Received?			

Name		20____	20____	20____
Address	Sent?			
	Received?			

Email		20____	20____	20____
Notes	Sent?			
	Received?			

Name		20____	20____	20____
Address	Sent?			
	Received?			

Email		20____	20____	20____
Notes	Sent?			
	Received?			

Name		20____	20____	20____
Address	Sent?			
	Received?			

Email		20____	20____	20____
Notes	Sent?			
	Received?			

Q

Name		20____	20____	20____
Address	Sent?			
	Received?			
Email		20____	20____	20____
Notes	Sent?			
	Received?			

Name		20____	20____	20____
Address	Sent?			
	Received?			
Email		20____	20____	20____
Notes	Sent?			
	Received?			

Name		20____	20____	20____
Address	Sent?			
	Received?			
Email		20____	20____	20____
Notes	Sent?			
	Received?			

Name		20____	20____	20____
Address	Sent?			
	Received?			
Email		20____	20____	20____
Notes	Sent?			
	Received?			

Q

Name		20___	20___	20___
Address	Sent?			
	Received?			
Email		20___	20___	20___
Notes	Sent?			
	Received?			

Name		20___	20___	20___
Address	Sent?			
	Received?			
Email		20___	20___	20___
Notes	Sent?			
	Received?			

Name		20___	20___	20___
Address	Sent?			
	Received?			
Email		20___	20___	20___
Notes	Sent?			
	Received?			

Name		20___	20___	20___
Address	Sent?			
	Received?			
Email		20___	20___	20___
Notes	Sent?			
	Received?			

Name		20___	20___	20___
Address	Sent?			
	Received?			
Email		20___	20___	20___
Notes	Sent?			
	Received?			

Name		20___	20___	20___
Address	Sent?			
	Received?			
Email		20___	20___	20___
Notes	Sent?			
	Received?			

Name		20___	20___	20___
Address	Sent?			
	Received?			
Email		20___	20___	20___
Notes	Sent?			
	Received?			

Name		20___	20___	20___
Address	Sent?			
	Received?			
Email		20___	20___	20___
Notes	Sent?			
	Received?			

Q

Name		20_____	20_____	20_____
Address	Sent?			
	Received?			
Email		20_____	20_____	20_____
Notes	Sent?			
	Received?			

Name		20_____	20_____	20_____
Address	Sent?			
	Received?			
Email		20_____	20_____	20_____
Notes	Sent?			
	Received?			

Name		20_____	20_____	20_____
Address	Sent?			
	Received?			
Email		20_____	20_____	20_____
Notes	Sent?			
	Received?			

Name		20_____	20_____	20_____
Address	Sent?			
	Received?			
Email		20_____	20_____	20_____
Notes	Sent?			
	Received?			

Q

Name		20___	20___	20___
Address	Sent?			
	Received?			
Email		20___	20___	20___
Notes	Sent?			
	Received?			

Name		20___	20___	20___
Address	Sent?			
	Received?			
Email		20___	20___	20___
Notes	Sent?			
	Received?			

Name		20___	20___	20___
Address	Sent?			
	Received?			
Email		20___	20___	20___
Notes	Sent?			
	Received?			

Name		20___	20___	20___
Address	Sent?			
	Received?			
Email		20___	20___	20___
Notes	Sent?			
	Received?			

R

Name		20___	20___	20___
Address	Sent?			
	Received?			

Email		20___	20___	20___
Notes	Sent?			
	Received?			

Name		20___	20___	20___
Address	Sent?			
	Received?			

Email		20___	20___	20___
Notes	Sent?			
	Received?			

Name		20___	20___	20___
Address	Sent?			
	Received?			

Email		20___	20___	20___
Notes	Sent?			
	Received?			

Name		20___	20___	20___
Address	Sent?			
	Received?			

Email		20___	20___	20___
Notes	Sent?			
	Received?			

Name		20____	20____	20____
Address	Sent?			
	Received?			
Email		20____	20____	20____
Notes	Sent?			
	Received?			

Name		20____	20____	20____
Address	Sent?			
	Received?			
Email		20____	20____	20____
Notes	Sent?			
	Received?			

Name		20____	20____	20____
Address	Sent?			
	Received?			
Email		20____	20____	20____
Notes	Sent?			
	Received?			

Name		20____	20____	20____
Address	Sent?			
	Received?			
Email		20____	20____	20____
Notes	Sent?			
	Received?			

R

Name		20____	20____	20____
Address	Sent?			
	Received?			
Email		20____	20____	20____
Notes	Sent?			
	Received?			

Name		20____	20____	20____
Address	Sent?			
	Received?			
Email		20____	20____	20____
Notes	Sent?			
	Received?			

Name		20____	20____	20____
Address	Sent?			
	Received?			
Email		20____	20____	20____
Notes	Sent?			
	Received?			

Name		20____	20____	20____
Address	Sent?			
	Received?			
Email		20____	20____	20____
Notes	Sent?			
	Received?			

Name		20____	20____	20____
Address	Sent?			
	Received?			
Email		20____	20____	20____
Notes	Sent?			
	Received?			

Name		20____	20____	20____
Address	Sent?			
	Received?			
Email		20____	20____	20____
Notes	Sent?			
	Received?			

Name		20____	20____	20____
Address	Sent?			
	Received?			
Email		20____	20____	20____
Notes	Sent?			
	Received?			

Name		20____	20____	20____
Address	Sent?			
	Received?			
Email		20____	20____	20____
Notes	Sent?			
	Received?			

R

Name		20____	20____	20____
Address	Sent?			
	Received?			
Email		20____	20____	20____
Notes	Sent?			
	Received?			

Name		20____	20____	20____
Address	Sent?			
	Received?			
Email		20____	20____	20____
Notes	Sent?			
	Received?			

Name		20____	20____	20____
Address	Sent?			
	Received?			
Email		20____	20____	20____
Notes	Sent?			
	Received?			

Name		20____	20____	20____
Address	Sent?			
	Received?			
Email		20____	20____	20____
Notes	Sent?			
	Received?			

Name		20____	20____	20____
Address	Sent?			
	Received?			
Email		20____	20____	20____
Notes	Sent?			
	Received?			

Name		20____	20____	20____
Address	Sent?			
	Received?			
Email		20____	20____	20____
Notes	Sent?			
	Received?			

Name		20____	20____	20____
Address	Sent?			
	Received?			
Email		20____	20____	20____
Notes	Sent?			
	Received?			

Name		20____	20____	20____
Address	Sent?			
	Received?			
Email		20____	20____	20____
Notes	Sent?			
	Received?			

S

Name		20____	20____	20____
Address	Sent?			
	Received?			
Email		20____	20____	20____
Notes	Sent?			
	Received?			

Name		20____	20____	20____
Address	Sent?			
	Received?			
Email		20____	20____	20____
Notes	Sent?			
	Received?			

Name		20____	20____	20____
Address	Sent?			
	Received?			
Email		20____	20____	20____
Notes	Sent?			
	Received?			

Name		20____	20____	20____
Address	Sent?			
	Received?			
Email		20____	20____	20____
Notes	Sent?			
	Received?			

Name		20____	20____	20____
Address	Sent?			
	Received?			
Email		20____	20____	20____
Notes	Sent?			
	Received?			

Name		20____	20____	20____
Address	Sent?			
	Received?			
Email		20____	20____	20____
Notes	Sent?			
	Received?			

Name		20____	20____	20____
Address	Sent?			
	Received?			
Email		20____	20____	20____
Notes	Sent?			
	Received?			

Name		20____	20____	20____
Address	Sent?			
	Received?			
Email		20____	20____	20____
Notes	Sent?			
	Received?			

S

Name	20___	20___	20___
Address	Sent?			
	Received?			

Email	20___	20___	20___
Notes	Sent?			
	Received?			

Name	20___	20___	20___
Address	Sent?			
	Received?			

Email	20___	20___	20___
Notes	Sent?			
	Received?			

Name	20___	20___	20___
Address	Sent?			
	Received?			

Email	20___	20___	20___
Notes	Sent?			
	Received?			

Name	20___	20___	20___
Address	Sent?			
	Received?			

Email	20___	20___	20___
Notes	Sent?			
	Received?			

Name		20____	20____	20____
Address	Sent?			
	Received?			
Email		20____	20____	20____
Notes	Sent?			
	Received?			

Name		20____	20____	20____
Address	Sent?			
	Received?			
Email		20____	20____	20____
Notes	Sent?			
	Received?			

Name		20____	20____	20____
Address	Sent?			
	Received?			
Email		20____	20____	20____
Notes	Sent?			
	Received?			

Name		20____	20____	20____
Address	Sent?			
	Received?			
Email		20____	20____	20____
Notes	Sent?			
	Received?			

S

Name		20___	20___	20___
Address	Sent?			
	Received?			
Email		20___	20___	20___
Notes	Sent?			
	Received?			

Name		20___	20___	20___
Address	Sent?			
	Received?			
Email		20___	20___	20___
Notes	Sent?			
	Received?			

Name		20___	20___	20___
Address	Sent?			
	Received?			
Email		20___	20___	20___
Notes	Sent?			
	Received?			

Name		20___	20___	20___
Address	Sent?			
	Received?			
Email		20___	20___	20___
Notes	Sent?			
	Received?			

S

Name		20____	20____	20____
Address	Sent?			
	Received?			
Email		20____	20____	20____
Notes	Sent?			
	Received?			

Name		20____	20____	20____
Address	Sent?			
	Received?			
Email		20____	20____	20____
Notes	Sent?			
	Received?			

Name		20____	20____	20____
Address	Sent?			
	Received?			
Email		20____	20____	20____
Notes	Sent?			
	Received?			

Name		20____	20____	20____
Address	Sent?			
	Received?			
Email		20____	20____	20____
Notes	Sent?			
	Received?			

T

		20____	20____	20____
Name				
Address	Sent?			
	Received?			
		20____	20____	20____
Email				
Notes	Sent?			
	Received?			

		20____	20____	20____
Name				
Address	Sent?			
	Received?			
		20____	20____	20____
Email				
Notes	Sent?			
	Received?			

		20____	20____	20____
Name				
Address	Sent?			
	Received?			
		20____	20____	20____
Email				
Notes	Sent?			
	Received?			

		20____	20____	20____
Name				
Address	Sent?			
	Received?			
		20____	20____	20____
Email				
Notes	Sent?			
	Received?			

T

	20___	20___	20___
Name			
Address	Sent?			
	Received?			

	20___	20___	20___
Email			
Notes	Sent?			
	Received?			

	20___	20___	20___
Name			
Address	Sent?			
	Received?			

	20___	20___	20___
Email			
Notes	Sent?			
	Received?			

	20___	20___	20___
Name			
Address	Sent?			
	Received?			

	20___	20___	20___
Email			
Notes	Sent?			
	Received?			

	20___	20___	20___
Name			
Address	Sent?			
	Received?			

	20___	20___	20___
Email			
Notes	Sent?			
	Received?			

T

Name		20____	20____	20____
Address	Sent?			
	Received?			
Email		20____	20____	20____
Notes	Sent?			
	Received?			

Name		20____	20____	20____
Address	Sent?			
	Received?			
Email		20____	20____	20____
Notes	Sent?			
	Received?			

Name		20____	20____	20____
Address	Sent?			
	Received?			
Email		20____	20____	20____
Notes	Sent?			
	Received?			

Name		20____	20____	20____
Address	Sent?			
	Received?			
Email		20____	20____	20____
Notes	Sent?			
	Received?			

T

Name		20____	20____	20____
Address	Sent?			
	Received?			
Email		20____	20____	20____
Notes	Sent?			
	Received?			

Name		20____	20____	20____
Address	Sent?			
	Received?			
Email		20____	20____	20____
Notes	Sent?			
	Received?			

Name		20____	20____	20____
Address	Sent?			
	Received?			
Email		20____	20____	20____
Notes	Sent?			
	Received?			

Name		20____	20____	20____
Address	Sent?			
	Received?			
Email		20____	20____	20____
Notes	Sent?			
	Received?			

T

Name		20_____	20_____	20_____
Address	Sent?			
	Received?			

Email		20_____	20_____	20_____
Notes	Sent?			
	Received?			

Name		20_____	20_____	20_____
Address	Sent?			
	Received?			

Email		20_____	20_____	20_____
Notes	Sent?			
	Received?			

Name		20_____	20_____	20_____
Address	Sent?			
	Received?			

Email		20_____	20_____	20_____
Notes	Sent?			
	Received?			

Name		20_____	20_____	20_____
Address	Sent?			
	Received?			

Email		20_____	20_____	20_____
Notes	Sent?			
	Received?			

T

Name		20___	20___	20___
Address	Sent?			
	Received?			
Email		20___	20___	20___
Notes	Sent?			
	Received?			

Name		20___	20___	20___
Address	Sent?			
	Received?			
Email		20___	20___	20___
Notes	Sent?			
	Received?			

Name		20___	20___	20___
Address	Sent?			
	Received?			
Email		20___	20___	20___
Notes	Sent?			
	Received?			

Name		20___	20___	20___
Address	Sent?			
	Received?			
Email		20___	20___	20___
Notes	Sent?			
	Received?			

U

		20____	20____	20____
Name				
Address	Sent?			
	Received?			

		20____	20____	20____
Email				
Notes	Sent?			
	Received?			

		20____	20____	20____
Name				
Address	Sent?			
	Received?			

		20____	20____	20____
Email				
Notes	Sent?			
	Received?			

		20____	20____	20____
Name				
Address	Sent?			
	Received?			

		20____	20____	20____
Email				
Notes	Sent?			
	Received?			

		20____	20____	20____
Name				
Address	Sent?			
	Received?			

		20____	20____	20____
Email				
Notes	Sent?			
	Received?			

Name		20____	20____	20____
Address	Sent?			
	Received?			
Email		20____	20____	20____
Notes	Sent?			
	Received?			

Name		20____	20____	20____
Address	Sent?			
	Received?			
Email		20____	20____	20____
Notes	Sent?			
	Received?			

Name		20____	20____	20____
Address	Sent?			
	Received?			
Email		20____	20____	20____
Notes	Sent?			
	Received?			

Name		20____	20____	20____
Address	Sent?			
	Received?			
Email		20____	20____	20____
Notes	Sent?			
	Received?			

U

Name		20___	20___	20___
Address	Sent?			
	Received?			
Email		20___	20___	20___
Notes	Sent?			
	Received?			

Name		20___	20___	20___
Address	Sent?			
	Received?			
Email		20___	20___	20___
Notes	Sent?			
	Received?			

Name		20___	20___	20___
Address	Sent?			
	Received?			
Email		20___	20___	20___
Notes	Sent?			
	Received?			

Name		20___	20___	20___
Address	Sent?			
	Received?			
Email		20___	20___	20___
Notes	Sent?			
	Received?			

U

Name		20___	20___	20___
Address	Sent?			
	Received?			
Email		20___	20___	20___
Notes	Sent?			
	Received?			

Name		20___	20___	20___
Address	Sent?			
	Received?			
Email		20___	20___	20___
Notes	Sent?			
	Received?			

Name		20___	20___	20___
Address	Sent?			
	Received?			
Email		20___	20___	20___
Notes	Sent?			
	Received?			

Name		20___	20___	20___
Address	Sent?			
	Received?			
Email		20___	20___	20___
Notes	Sent?			
	Received?			

U

Name		20___	20___	20___
Address	Sent?			
	Received?			

Email		20___	20___	20___
Notes	Sent?			
	Received?			

Name		20___	20___	20___
Address	Sent?			
	Received?			

Email		20___	20___	20___
Notes	Sent?			
	Received?			

Name		20___	20___	20___
Address	Sent?			
	Received?			

Email		20___	20___	20___
Notes	Sent?			
	Received?			

Name		20___	20___	20___
Address	Sent?			
	Received?			

Email		20___	20___	20___
Notes	Sent?			
	Received?			

Name		20____	20____	20____
Address	Sent?			
	Received?			
Email		20____	20____	20____
Notes	Sent?			
	Received?			

Name		20____	20____	20____
Address	Sent?			
	Received?			
Email		20____	20____	20____
Notes	Sent?			
	Received?			

Name		20____	20____	20____
Address	Sent?			
	Received?			
Email		20____	20____	20____
Notes	Sent?			
	Received?			

Name		20____	20____	20____
Address	Sent?			
	Received?			
Email		20____	20____	20____
Notes	Sent?			
	Received?			

V

Name		20____	20____	20____
Address	Sent?			
	Received?			

Email		20____	20____	20____
Notes	Sent?			
	Received?			

Name		20____	20____	20____
Address	Sent?			
	Received?			

Email		20____	20____	20____
Notes	Sent?			
	Received?			

Name		20____	20____	20____
Address	Sent?			
	Received?			

Email		20____	20____	20____
Notes	Sent?			
	Received?			

Name		20____	20____	20____
Address	Sent?			
	Received?			

Email		20____	20____	20____
Notes	Sent?			
	Received?			

V

Name		20____	20____	20____
Address	Sent?			
	Received?			
Email		20____	20____	20____
Notes	Sent?			
	Received?			

Name		20____	20____	20____
Address	Sent?			
	Received?			
Email		20____	20____	20____
Notes	Sent?			
	Received?			

Name		20____	20____	20____
Address	Sent?			
	Received?			
Email		20____	20____	20____
Notes	Sent?			
	Received?			

Name		20____	20____	20____
Address	Sent?			
	Received?			
Email		20____	20____	20____
Notes	Sent?			
	Received?			

V

Name		20____	20____	20____
Address	Sent?			
	Received?			
Email		20____	20____	20____
Notes	Sent?			
	Received?			

Name		20____	20____	20____
Address	Sent?			
	Received?			
Email		20____	20____	20____
Notes	Sent?			
	Received?			

Name		20____	20____	20____
Address	Sent?			
	Received?			
Email		20____	20____	20____
Notes	Sent?			
	Received?			

Name		20____	20____	20____
Address	Sent?			
	Received?			
Email		20____	20____	20____
Notes	Sent?			
	Received?			

V

Name

Address		20___	20___	20___
	Sent?			
	Received?			

Email		20___	20___	20___
Notes	Sent?			
	Received?			

Name

Address		20___	20___	20___
	Sent?			
	Received?			

Email		20___	20___	20___
Notes	Sent?			
	Received?			

Name

Address		20___	20___	20___
	Sent?			
	Received?			

Email		20___	20___	20___
Notes	Sent?			
	Received?			

Name

Address		20___	20___	20___
	Sent?			
	Received?			

Email		20___	20___	20___
Notes	Sent?			
	Received?			

V

Name		20____	20____	20____
Address	Sent?			
	Received?			
Email		20____	20____	20____
Notes	Sent?			
	Received?			

Name		20____	20____	20____
Address	Sent?			
	Received?			
Email		20____	20____	20____
Notes	Sent?			
	Received?			

Name		20____	20____	20____
Address	Sent?			
	Received?			
Email		20____	20____	20____
Notes	Sent?			
	Received?			

Name		20____	20____	20____
Address	Sent?			
	Received?			
Email		20____	20____	20____
Notes	Sent?			
	Received?			

Name		20____	20____	20____
Address	Sent?			
	Received?			
Email		20____	20____	20____
Notes	Sent?			
	Received?			

Name		20____	20____	20____
Address	Sent?			
	Received?			
Email		20____	20____	20____
Notes	Sent?			
	Received?			

Name		20____	20____	20____
Address	Sent?			
	Received?			
Email		20____	20____	20____
Notes	Sent?			
	Received?			

Name		20____	20____	20____
Address	Sent?			
	Received?			
Email		20____	20____	20____
Notes	Sent?			
	Received?			

Name		20____	20____	20____
Address	Sent?			
	Received?			
Email		20____	20____	20____
Notes	Sent?			
	Received?			

Name		20____	20____	20____
Address	Sent?			
	Received?			
Email		20____	20____	20____
Notes	Sent?			
	Received?			

Name		20____	20____	20____
Address	Sent?			
	Received?			
Email		20____	20____	20____
Notes	Sent?			
	Received?			

Name		20____	20____	20____
Address	Sent?			
	Received?			
Email		20____	20____	20____
Notes	Sent?			
	Received?			

Name

Address   20_____   20_____   20_____

Sent?

Received?

Email   20_____   20_____   20_____

Notes

Sent?

Received?

Name

Address   20_____   20_____   20_____

Sent?

Received?

Email   20_____   20_____   20_____

Notes

Sent?

Received?

Name

Address   20_____   20_____   20_____

Sent?

Received?

Email   20_____   20_____   20_____

Notes

Sent?

Received?

Name

Address   20_____   20_____   20_____

Sent?

Received?

Email   20_____   20_____   20_____

Notes

Sent?

Received?

W

Name		20____	20____	20____
Address	Sent?			
	Received?			
Email		20____	20____	20____
Notes	Sent?			
	Received?			

Name		20____	20____	20____
Address	Sent?			
	Received?			
Email		20____	20____	20____
Notes	Sent?			
	Received?			

Name		20____	20____	20____
Address	Sent?			
	Received?			
Email		20____	20____	20____
Notes	Sent?			
	Received?			

Name		20____	20____	20____
Address	Sent?			
	Received?			
Email		20____	20____	20____
Notes	Sent?			
	Received?			

W

Name _____ 20____ 20____ 20____

Address _____ Sent?

Received?

Email _____ 20____ 20____ 20____

Notes _____ Sent?

Received?

Name _____ 20____ 20____ 20____

Address _____ Sent?

Received?

Email _____ 20____ 20____ 20____

Notes _____ Sent?

Received?

Name _____ 20____ 20____ 20____

Address _____ Sent?

Received?

Email _____ 20____ 20____ 20____

Notes _____ Sent?

Received?

Name _____ 20____ 20____ 20____

Address _____ Sent?

Received?

Email _____ 20____ 20____ 20____

Notes _____ Sent?

Received?

W

Name	20___	20___	20___
Address Sent?			
Received?			

Email	20___	20___	20___
Notes Sent?			
Received?			

Name	20___	20___	20___
Address Sent?			
Received?			

Email	20___	20___	20___
Notes Sent?			
Received?			

Name	20___	20___	20___
Address Sent?			
Received?			

Email	20___	20___	20___
Notes Sent?			
Received?			

Name	20___	20___	20___
Address Sent?			
Received?			

Email	20___	20___	20___
Notes Sent?			
Received?			

Name		20____	20____	20____
Address	Sent?			
	Received?			
Email		20____	20____	20____
Notes	Sent?			
	Received?			

Name		20____	20____	20____
Address	Sent?			
	Received?			
Email		20____	20____	20____
Notes	Sent?			
	Received?			

Name		20____	20____	20____
Address	Sent?			
	Received?			
Email		20____	20____	20____
Notes	Sent?			
	Received?			

Name		20____	20____	20____
Address	Sent?			
	Received?			
Email		20____	20____	20____
Notes	Sent?			
	Received?			

X

Name		20___	20___	20___
Address	Sent?			
	Received?			
Email		20___	20___	20___
Notes	Sent?			
	Received?			

Name		20___	20___	20___
Address	Sent?			
	Received?			
Email		20___	20___	20___
Notes	Sent?			
	Received?			

Name		20___	20___	20___
Address	Sent?			
	Received?			
Email		20___	20___	20___
Notes	Sent?			
	Received?			

Name		20___	20___	20___
Address	Sent?			
	Received?			
Email		20___	20___	20___
Notes	Sent?			
	Received?			

Name		20____	20____	20____
Address	Sent?			
	Received?			
Email		20____	20____	20____
Notes	Sent?			
	Received?			

Name		20____	20____	20____
Address	Sent?			
	Received?			
Email		20____	20____	20____
Notes	Sent?			
	Received?			

Name		20____	20____	20____
Address	Sent?			
	Received?			
Email		20____	20____	20____
Notes	Sent?			
	Received?			

Name		20____	20____	20____
Address	Sent?			
	Received?			
Email		20____	20____	20____
Notes	Sent?			
	Received?			

X

Name		20____	20____	20____
Address	Sent?			
	Received?			
Email		20____	20____	20____
Notes	Sent?			
	Received?			

Name		20____	20____	20____
Address	Sent?			
	Received?			
Email		20____	20____	20____
Notes	Sent?			
	Received?			

Name		20____	20____	20____
Address	Sent?			
	Received?			
Email		20____	20____	20____
Notes	Sent?			
	Received?			

Name		20____	20____	20____
Address	Sent?			
	Received?			
Email		20____	20____	20____
Notes	Sent?			
	Received?			

Name		20____	20____	20____
Address	Sent?			
	Received?			
Email		20____	20____	20____
Notes	Sent?			
	Received?			

Name		20____	20____	20____
Address	Sent?			
	Received?			
Email		20____	20____	20____
Notes	Sent?			
	Received?			

Name		20____	20____	20____
Address	Sent?			
	Received?			
Email		20____	20____	20____
Notes	Sent?			
	Received?			

Name		20____	20____	20____
Address	Sent?			
	Received?			
Email		20____	20____	20____
Notes	Sent?			
	Received?			

X

Name		20____	20____	20____
Address	Sent?			
	Received?			
Email		20____	20____	20____
Notes	Sent?			
	Received?			

Name		20____	20____	20____
Address	Sent?			
	Received?			
Email		20____	20____	20____
Notes	Sent?			
	Received?			

Name		20____	20____	20____
Address	Sent?			
	Received?			
Email		20____	20____	20____
Notes	Sent?			
	Received?			

Name		20____	20____	20____
Address	Sent?			
	Received?			
Email		20____	20____	20____
Notes	Sent?			
	Received?			

X

Name		20____	20____	20____
Address	Sent?			
	Received?			
Email		20____	20____	20____
Notes	Sent?			
	Received?			

Name		20____	20____	20____
Address	Sent?			
	Received?			
Email		20____	20____	20____
Notes	Sent?			
	Received?			

Name		20____	20____	20____
Address	Sent?			
	Received?			
Email		20____	20____	20____
Notes	Sent?			
	Received?			

Name		20____	20____	20____
Address	Sent?			
	Received?			
Email		20____	20____	20____
Notes	Sent?			
	Received?			

Y

Name		20____	20____	20____
Address	Sent?			
	Received?			
Email		20____	20____	20____
Notes	Sent?			
	Received?			

Name		20____	20____	20____
Address	Sent?			
	Received?			
Email		20____	20____	20____
Notes	Sent?			
	Received?			

Name		20____	20____	20____
Address	Sent?			
	Received?			
Email		20____	20____	20____
Notes	Sent?			
	Received?			

Name		20____	20____	20____
Address	Sent?			
	Received?			
Email		20____	20____	20____
Notes	Sent?			
	Received?			

Y

		20____	20____	20____
Name				
Address	Sent?			
	Received?			
Email		20____	20____	20____
Notes	Sent?			
	Received?			

		20____	20____	20____
Name				
Address	Sent?			
	Received?			
Email		20____	20____	20____
Notes	Sent?			
	Received?			

		20____	20____	20____
Name				
Address	Sent?			
	Received?			
Email		20____	20____	20____
Notes	Sent?			
	Received?			

		20____	20____	20____
Name				
Address	Sent?			
	Received?			
Email		20____	20____	20____
Notes	Sent?			
	Received?			

Y

Name		20___	20___	20___
Address	Sent?			
	Received?			
Email		20___	20___	20___
Notes	Sent?			
	Received?			

Name		20___	20___	20___
Address	Sent?			
	Received?			
Email		20___	20___	20___
Notes	Sent?			
	Received?			

Name		20___	20___	20___
Address	Sent?			
	Received?			
Email		20___	20___	20___
Notes	Sent?			
	Received?			

Name		20___	20___	20___
Address	Sent?			
	Received?			
Email		20___	20___	20___
Notes	Sent?			
	Received?			

Y

		20____	20____	20____
Name				
Address	Sent?			
	Received?			
Email		20____	20____	20____
Notes	Sent?			
	Received?			

		20____	20____	20____
Name				
Address	Sent?			
	Received?			
Email		20____	20____	20____
Notes	Sent?			
	Received?			

		20____	20____	20____
Name				
Address	Sent?			
	Received?			
Email		20____	20____	20____
Notes	Sent?			
	Received?			

		20____	20____	20____
Name				
Address	Sent?			
	Received?			
Email		20____	20____	20____
Notes	Sent?			
	Received?			

Y

		20___	20___	20___
Name				
Address	Sent?			
	Received?			

		20___	20___	20___
Email				
Notes	Sent?			
	Received?			

		20___	20___	20___
Name				
Address	Sent?			
	Received?			

		20___	20___	20___
Email				
Notes	Sent?			
	Received?			

		20___	20___	20___
Name				
Address	Sent?			
	Received?			

		20___	20___	20___
Email				
Notes	Sent?			
	Received?			

		20___	20___	20___
Name				
Address	Sent?			
	Received?			

		20___	20___	20___
Email				
Notes	Sent?			
	Received?			

Y

Name		20____	20____	20____
Address	Sent?			
	Received?			
Email		20____	20____	20____
Notes	Sent?			
	Received?			

Name		20____	20____	20____
Address	Sent?			
	Received?			
Email		20____	20____	20____
Notes	Sent?			
	Received?			

Name		20____	20____	20____
Address	Sent?			
	Received?			
Email		20____	20____	20____
Notes	Sent?			
	Received?			

Name		20____	20____	20____
Address	Sent?			
	Received?			
Email		20____	20____	20____
Notes	Sent?			
	Received?			

Z

Name		20___	20___	20___
Address	Sent?			
	Received?			
Email		20___	20___	20___
Notes	Sent?			
	Received?			

Name		20___	20___	20___
Address	Sent?			
	Received?			
Email		20___	20___	20___
Notes	Sent?			
	Received?			

Name		20___	20___	20___
Address	Sent?			
	Received?			
Email		20___	20___	20___
Notes	Sent?			
	Received?			

Name		20___	20___	20___
Address	Sent?			
	Received?			
Email		20___	20___	20___
Notes	Sent?			
	Received?			

Name		20___	20___	20___
Address	Sent?			
	Received?			
Email		20___	20___	20___
Notes	Sent?			
	Received?			

Name		20___	20___	20___
Address	Sent?			
	Received?			
Email		20___	20___	20___
Notes	Sent?			
	Received?			

Name		20___	20___	20___
Address	Sent?			
	Received?			
Email		20___	20___	20___
Notes	Sent?			
	Received?			

Name		20___	20___	20___
Address	Sent?			
	Received?			
Email		20___	20___	20___
Notes	Sent?			
	Received?			

Z

Name		20____	20____	20____
Address	Sent?			
	Received?			
Email		20____	20____	20____
Notes	Sent?			
	Received?			

Name		20____	20____	20____
Address	Sent?			
	Received?			
Email		20____	20____	20____
Notes	Sent?			
	Received?			

Name		20____	20____	20____
Address	Sent?			
	Received?			
Email		20____	20____	20____
Notes	Sent?			
	Received?			

Name		20____	20____	20____
Address	Sent?			
	Received?			
Email		20____	20____	20____
Notes	Sent?			
	Received?			

Z

Name		20____	20____	20____
Address	Sent?			
	Received?			
Email		20____	20____	20____
Notes	Sent?			
	Received?			

Name		20____	20____	20____
Address	Sent?			
	Received?			
Email		20____	20____	20____
Notes	Sent?			
	Received?			

Name		20____	20____	20____
Address	Sent?			
	Received?			
Email		20____	20____	20____
Notes	Sent?			
	Received?			

Name		20____	20____	20____
Address	Sent?			
	Received?			
Email		20____	20____	20____
Notes	Sent?			
	Received?			

Z

Name		20___	20___	20___
Address	Sent?			
	Received?			

Email		20___	20___	20___
Notes	Sent?			
	Received?			

Name		20___	20___	20___
Address	Sent?			
	Received?			

Email		20___	20___	20___
Notes	Sent?			
	Received?			

Name		20___	20___	20___
Address	Sent?			
	Received?			

Email		20___	20___	20___
Notes	Sent?			
	Received?			

Name		20___	20___	20___
Address	Sent?			
	Received?			

Email		20___	20___	20___
Notes	Sent?			
	Received?			

Z

Name		20___	20___	20___
Address	Sent?			
	Received?			
Email		20___	20___	20___
Notes	Sent?			
	Received?			

Name		20___	20___	20___
Address	Sent?			
	Received?			
Email		20___	20___	20___
Notes	Sent?			
	Received?			

Name		20___	20___	20___
Address	Sent?			
	Received?			
Email		20___	20___	20___
Notes	Sent?			
	Received?			

Name		20___	20___	20___
Address	Sent?			
	Received?			
Email		20___	20___	20___
Notes	Sent?			
	Received?			

NOTES

NOTES

NOTES

Made in the USA
Middletown, DE
21 October 2023

41208643R00091